GOD'S PLAN FOR MARRIAGE & FAMILY

Word of God Ministries
Bob & Jean Shaw

Trilogy Christian Publishers
A Wholly Owned Subsidiary of Trinity Broadcasting Network
2442 Michelle Drive
Tustin, CA 92780

Copyright © 2023 by Bob & Jean Shaw.

Unless otherwise indicated, all scripture quotations are from the New King James Version®. Copyright © 1982 by Thomas Nelson. Used by permission. All rights reserved

Scripture quotations marked AMP are taken from the Amplified® Bible (AMP), Copyright © 2015 by The Lockman Foundation. Used by permission. www.Lockman.org.

Scripture quotations marked NLT are taken from the Holy Bible, New Living Translation, copyright © 1996, 2004, 2015 by Tyndale House Foundation. Used by permission of Tyndale House Publishers, Inc., Carol Stream, Illinois 60188. All rights reserved.

Scriptures marked KJV are taken from the King James Version. Public domain.

All rights reserved, including the right to reproduce this book or portions thereof in any form whatsoever.

For information, address Trilogy Christian Publishing

Rights Department, 2442 Michelle Drive, Tustin, Ca 92780.

Trilogy Christian Publishing/ TBN and colophon are trademarks of Trinity Broadcasting Network.

For information about special discounts for bulk purchases, please contact Trilogy Christian Publishing.

Trilogy Disclaimer: The views and content expressed in this book are those of the author and may not necessarily reflect the views and doctrine of Trilogy Christian Publishing or the Trinity Broadcasting Network.

10 9 8 7 6 5 4 3 2 1

Library of Congress Cataloging-in-Publication Data is available.

ISBN 979-8-89041-377-2

ISBN 979-8-89041-378-9 (ebook)

"The Believers School of Training"

God's Plan
for
Marriage
&
Family

"For no other FOUNDATION can anyone lay than that which is laid, which is Jesus Christ"
1 Corinthians 3:11

Don't let the **Honey** out of the **Honeymoon**

WORD OF GOD MINISTRIES
Bob & Jean Shaw

Teacher/Evangelists
Certified Human Behavior Consultants

BECOMING BORN AGAIN (SAVED) AND RECEIVING ETERNAL LIFE ACCORDING TO THE SCRIPTURES

a. John 3:16, For God so loved the world that He gave His only begotten Son, that whoever believes in Him (Jesus) should not perish but have everlasting life.
b. Romans 3:23, For all have sinned and fall short of the glory of God.
c. Romans 6:23, For the wages of sin death, but the gift of God is eternal life in Christ Jesus our Lord.
d. Acts 3:19, Repent therefore and be converted, that your sins may be blotted out, so that times of Refreshing may come from the presence of the Lord.
e. John 3:5-7, Jesus answered, "Most assuredly, I say to you unless one is born of water and the Spirit, he cannot enter the Kingdom of God. That which is born of the flesh is flesh, and that which is born of the Spirit is spirit. Do not marvel that I said to you, you **MUST be BORN AGAIN.**"
f. Romans 10:8-10, But what does it say? The word is near you, in your mouth and in your heart (that is the word of faith which we preach) that if you confess with your mouth the Lord Jesus and believe in your heart that God has raised Him (Jesus) from the dead you will be saved. For with the heart one believes unto righteousness, and with the mouth confession is made unto salvation.

PRAYER TO ACCEPT JESUS AS YOUR PERSONAL SAVIOR

Dear God, I confess my sins to you and believe that Jesus is the way I can be reconciled to you, through His shed Blood on Calvary. I repent of my sin and ask you Jesus to forgive me of all my sins. I confess with my mouth You Lord Jesus as my personal Savior, and I believe in my heart that God raised You from the dead. Thank You for Washing my sins away with your shed blood, and giving me Eternal Life, and a home in Heaven one day,

In Jesus Name, I pray.

Table of Contents

Part I: Foundation and Order for Marriage 9
Part II: Communication 23
    Includes Communication Survey 23
Part III: Money 39
    Includes Financial Management Survey 39
Part IV: Sex in Marriage 61
Part V: Parents' Responsibility for Children 69

WORD OF GOD MINISTRIES
Bob and Jean Shaw

Word of God Ministries
Bob & Jean Shaw
Bible Teachers and Authors
Certified Human Behavior Consultants
https://www.kingdomtruth.net

 Bob and Jean Shaw offer an extensive exploration of the sacred institution of marriage, drawing from the timeless wisdom of the Bible in *God's Plan for Marriage and Family*. This excellent book stands as a beacon of hope and guidance for couples seeking a fulfilling and enduring marital journey.

 One remarkable aspect of this book is the author's own ongoing marital journey—a testament to the endurance and resilience of a committed marital bond. Having been married for an incredible sixty-one years, Bob and Jean Shaw bring a wealth of firsthand knowledge and understanding to the pages. Their wisdom shines through, offering a heartfelt perspective on the joys, challenges, and triumphs that accompany a lifelong partnership.

 This book not only offers practical advice but also invites readers to reflect on their own relationships, fostering a deeper appreciation for the sacred commitment of marriage. It reminds us that with faith, dedication, and the guidance of biblical wisdom, our unions can withstand the test of time.

 Whether you are newly engaged, celebrating a milestone anniversary, or walking through the trials of marriage, *God's Plan for Marriage and Family* is an invaluable companion. It illuminates the path toward a fulfilling, God-centered marriage, allowing us to forge a bond that echoes throughout eternity.

 It is an honor to endorse this book, knowing that its wisdom will continue to inspire and guide generations to come.

Warmest regards,
Matthew Austin
Kingdom Lights
https://www.kingdomlights.org

Bob and Jean Shaw's book, *God's Plan for Marriage and Family*, is an absolute gem that strikes the perfect balance between wisdom and warmth, reminding us not to let the "honey out of the honeymoon." With a profound exploration of the teachings within Scripture, this book is a treasure trove of insights. Whether you find yourself single, navigating the complexities of dating, standing on the brink of engagement, or have celebrated years of marriage, *God's Plan for Marriage and Family* is an invaluable guide. I wholeheartedly recommend it to everyone, as it beautifully weaves the timeless wisdom of Scripture into the fabric of our modern lives.

Adam Louks
Oasis Church
https://www.oasischurchmi.org/

Part I: Foundation and Order for Marriage

I. Do we want to know the *Truth*?

   A. "And you shall **KNOW** the *truth* and the *truth* shall set (**MAKE**) you free" (John 8:32).

   B. "Sanctify [cleanse] them by Your *truth*. Your word is *truth*" (John 17:17).

   C. "For the word of God *is* living and powerful, and sharper than any two-edged sword, piercing even to the division of soul and spirit, and of joints and marrow, and is a discerner of the thoughts and intents of the heart" (Hebrews 4:12).

   D. "My people are destroyed for lack of knowledge. Because you have rejected knowledge, I also will reject you from being priest for Me; Because you have forgotten the law of your God, I also will forget your children" (Hosea 4:6).

      1. Correct knowledge and information can stop us from perishing.

   E. What are traditions of man? The handing down of beliefs, opinions, customs, stories, information, and instructions from generation to generation.

   Where man's traditions exist, contrary to the *Truth*, it will make *God's Word* ineffective and produce defeat.

"And in vain they worship me, Teaching *as* doctrines the commandments of men. For laying aside the commandment of God, you hold the tradition of men— the washing of pitchers and cups: and many other such like things you do. He said to them, '*All too* well you reject the commandment of God, that you may keep your tradition… making the word of God of no effect through your tradition which you have handed down. And many such things you do'" (Mark 7:7–9,13).

F. God watches over *His Word* to perform it.

"Then the LORD said to me, 'You have seen well, for I am ready to perform My word'" (Jeremiah 1:12).

G. *God's Word* will not return void.

"So shall My word be that goes forth from My mouth; It shall not return to Me void, But it shall accomplish what I please, And it shall prosper *in the thing* for which I sent it" (Isaiah 55:11).

H. Happy is the man who finds wisdom, And the man who gains understanding; For her proceeds are better than the profits of silver, And her gain than fine gold. She is more precious than rubies, And all the things you may desire cannot compare with her. Length of days is in her right hand, In her left hand riches and honor. Her ways are ways of pleasantness, And all her paths are peace. She is a tree of life to those who take hold of her, And happy are all who retain her. The LORD by wisdom founded the earth; By understanding He established the heavens; By His knowledge the depths were broken up, And clouds drop down the dew. My son, let them not depart from your eyes— Keep sound wisdom and discretion; So they will be life to your soul And grace to your neck. Then you will walk safely in your way, And your foot will not stumble. When you lie down, you will not be afraid; Yes, you will lie down and your sleep will be sweet. Do not be afraid of sudden terror, Nor of trouble from the wicked when it comes; For the LORD will be your confidence, And will keep your foot from being caught. Do not withhold good from those to whom it is due, When it is in the power of your hand to do so.

Proverbs 3:13–27

II. Who wants to destroy Marriages?

A. "The thief does not come except to steal, and to kill, and to destroy. I have come that they may have life, and that they may have it more abundantly" (John 10:10).

B. "Be sober, be vigilant; because your adversary the devil walks about like a roaring lion, seeking whom he may devour" (1 Peter 5:8).

C. We wrestle not against flesh and blood.

This generation has so many things that can affect marriage. Evil abounds everywhere. The Church of Jesus Christ has the answers and must be *Telling* and *Teaching the Truth.*

Finally, my brethren, be strong in the Lord and in the power of His might. Put on the whole armor of God, that you may be able to stand against the wiles of the devil. For we do not wrestle against flesh and blood, but against principalities, against powers, against the rulers of the darkness of this age, against spiritual hosts of wickedness in the heavenly places.

Ephesians 6:10–12 (KJV)

D. Then I heard a loud voice saying in heaven, "Now salvation, and strength, and the kingdom of our God, and the power of His Christ have come, for the accuser of our brethren, who accused them before our God day and night, has been cast down. And they overcame him by the blood of the Lamb AND by the word of their testimony, and they did not love their lives to the death."

Revelation 12:10–11

V. 10 - Satan is the accuser of the brethren.

V. 11 - They overcame the devil by the **blood of the lamb** AND **by the word of their testimony** (about the blood).

III. What is a family, house, or home?
A. Family - related people, father, mother, and children.
B. House - refers only to a building.
C. Home - refers to any place that is the center to one's family and affections.

IV. Let's look at the *Truth* about marriage in the beginning.
A. Then God said, "Let Us make man in Our image, according to Our likeness; let them have dominion over the fish of the sea, over the birds of the air, and over the cattle, over all the earth and over every creeping thing that creeps on the earth." So God created man in His own image; in the image of God He created him; male and female He created them. Then God blessed them, and God said to them, "Be fruitful and multiply; fill the earth and subdue it; have dominion over the fish of the sea, over the birds of the air, and over every living thing that moves on the earth."

Genesis 1:26–28

B. Leave father and mother and the two (man and woman) shall be one flesh.

And the LORD God said, "*It is* not good that man should be alone; I will make him a helper comparable to him." Out of the ground the LORD God formed every beast of the field and every bird of the air, and brought *them* to Adam to see what he would call them. And whatever Adam called each living creature, that *was* its name. So Adam gave names to all cattle, to the birds of the air, and to every beast of the field. But for Adam there was not found a helper comparable to him. And the LORD God caused a deep sleep to fall on Adam, and he slept; and He took one of his ribs, and closed up the flesh in its place. Then the rib which the LORD God had taken from man He made into a woman, and He brought her to the man. And Adam said, "This *is* now bone of my bones And flesh of my flesh; She shall be called Woman, Because she was taken out of Man." Therefore a man shall leave his father and mother and be joined to his wife, and they shall become one flesh.

Genesis 2:18–24

1. Where two agree there is power.

   "Again I say to you that if two of you agree on earth concerning anything that they ask, it will be done for them by My Father in heaven…" (Matthew 18:19).

2. Two are better than one.

   Two are better than one, because they have a good reward for their labor. For if they fall, one will lift up his companion. But woe to him who is alone when he falls. For he has no one to help him up.

Again, if two lie down together, they will keep warm; But how can one be warm alone? Though one may be overpowered by another, two can withstand him. And a threefold cord is not quickly broken.

Ecclesiastes 4:9–12

C. The two become one flesh.

And he answered and said unto them, "Have ye not read, that he which made them at the beginning made them male and female, And said, For this cause shall a man leave father and mother, and shall cleave to his wife: and they twain shall be one flesh?" Wherefore they are no more twain, but one flesh. What therefore God hath joined together, let not man put asunder.

Matthew 19:4–6 (KJV)

He replied, "Have you never read that He who created them from the beginning MADE THEM MALE AND FEMALE, and said, 'FOR THIS REASON A MAN SHALL LEAVE HIS FATHER AND MOTHER AND SHALL BE JOINED INSEPARABLY TO HIS WIFE, AND THE TWO SHALL BECOME ONE FLESH'? So they are no longer two, but one flesh. Therefore, what God has joined together, let no one separate."

Matthew 19:4–6 (AMP)

V. **God has a plan and order for marriage - Husband and Wife.**

A. God's order:

"But I want you to understand that Christ is the head (authority over) of every man, and man is the head of woman, and God is the head of Christ" (1 Corinthians 11:3, AMP).

B. God's formula and plan:

   …submitting to one another in the fear of God. Wives, submit to your own husbands, as to the Lord. For the husband is head of the wife, as also Christ is head of the church; and He is the Savior of the body. Therefore, just as the church is subject to Christ, so *let* the wives *be* to their own husbands in everything.

   Husbands, love your wives, just as Christ also loved the church and gave Himself for her, that He might sanctify and cleanse her with the washing of water by the word, that He might present her to Himself a glorious church, not having spot or wrinkle or any such thing, but that she should be holy and without blemish. So husbands ought to love their own wives as their own bodies; he who loves his wife loves himself. For no one ever hated his own flesh, but nourishes and cherishes it, just as the Lord *does* the church. For we are members of His body, of His flesh and of His bones. "For this reason a man shall leave his father and mother and be joined to his wife, and the two shall become one flesh." This is a great mystery, but I speak concerning Christ and the church. Nevertheless let each one of you in particular so love his own wife as himself, and let the wife *see* that she respects *her* husband.

   Ephesians 5:21–33

   1. V. 21 **"Submit yourselves to one another in the fear of God."**

   2. V. 22–24

   Wives submit to your own husbands, as to the Lord. For the husband Is head of the wife, as also Christ is head of the church; and He is the Savior of the body.

Therefore, just as the church is subject to Christ, so let the wives be to their own husbands in everything.

3. V. 25–28

Husbands love your wives, just as Christ also loved the church and Gave Himself for her, that He might sanctify and cleanse her with the washing of water by the word that He might present her to Himself a glorious church, not having spot or wrinkle or any such thing, but that she should be holy and without blemish. So husbands ought to love their own wives as their own bodies; he who loves his wife loves himself.

4. V. 25 **Wives' vitamin is LOVE.**

5. V. 33 **Husbands' vitamin is RESPECT.**

6. Good marriages don't just happen; it takes work and the Lord being the center focus of the marriage.

C. God's order for the family:

1. **"Christ"** - Seek God's Kingdom FIRST and all these things will be added unto you. Now if God so clothes the grass of the field, which today is, and tomorrow is thrown into the oven, will He not much more clothe you, O you of little faith? Therefore do not worry, saying, "What shall we eat?" or "What shall we drink?" or "What shall we wear?" For after all these things the Gentiles seek. For your heavenly Father knows that you need all these things. But seek first the kingdom of God and His righteousness, and all these things shall be added unto you.

Matthew 6:30–33

2. **"Husband"** - Husband is the head of the family under Christ.

"For the husband is head of the wife, as also Christ is head of the church; and He is the Savior of the body" (Ephesians 5:23).

a. "In the same way, you husbands, live with your wives in an understanding way [with great gentleness and tact, and with an intelligent regard for the marriage relationship], as with someone physically weaker, since she is a woman. Show her honor and respect as a fellow heir of the grace of life, so that your prayers will not be hindered or ineffective" (1 Peter 3:7, AMP).

- Men must keep their word to their wife and their children.

- Men must accept the responsibility for their actions.

- Men must be God wise, not street wise or even church wise, but God wise.

- When men have a healthy relationship with their Heavenly Father, they can have a good relationship with their wife and children.

- Men must accept their family role in Stewardship, Relationship, and Leadership.

- Maturity starts with responsibility, not age.

- Fathers must show Respect, Discipline/Love, and Value towards their children.

3. *"Wife"* - Wife is to guide the house.

"Therefore I desire that the younger widows marry, bear children, manage the house, give no opportunity to the adversary to speak reproachfully" (1 Timothy 5:14).

a. A word to wives:

Wives, likewise, be submissive to your own husbands, that even if some do not obey the word, they, without a word, may be won by the conduct of their wives, when they observe your chaste conduct accompanied by fear. Do not let your adornment be merely outward—arranging the hair, wearing gold, or putting on fine apparel—rather let it be the hidden person of the heart, with the incorruptible beauty of a gentle and quiet spirit, which is very precious in the sight of God. For in this manner, in former times, the holy women who trusted in God also adorned themselves, being submissive to their own husbands, as Sarah obeyed Abraham, calling him lord, whose daughters you are if you do good and are not afraid with any terror.

1 Peter 3:1–6

V. 1–2 A husband may be won by the chaste conduct of the wife.

V. 3–4 Wives let your adornment be of the hidden person of the heart, with the incorruptible beauty of a gentle and quiet spirit, very precious in God's sight.

V. 5–6 Wives submit to the leadership of your own husband.

b. A virtuous woman:

Who can find a virtuous wife? For her worth is far above rubies. The heart of her husband safely trusts her; So, he will have no lack of gain. She does him good and not evil All the days of her life. She seeks wool and flax, and willingly works with her hands. She is like the merchant ships; she brings her food from afar. She also rises while it is yet night, and provides food for her household, and a portion for her maidservants. She considers a field and buys it; From her profits she plants a vineyard. She girds herself with strength and strengthens her arms. She perceives that her merchandise is good, and her lamp does not go out by night. She stretches out her hands to the distaff, and her hand holds the spindle. She extends her hand to the poor, yes, she reaches out her hands to the needy. She is not afraid of snow for her household, for all her household is clothed with scarlet. She makes tapestry for herself; Her clothing is fine linen and purple. Her husband is known in the gates, when he sits among the elders of the land. She makes linen garments and sells them and supplies sashes for the merchants. Strength and honor are her clothing; She shall rejoice in time to come. She opens her mouth with wisdom, and on her tongue is the law of kindness. She watches over the ways of her household and does not eat the bread of idleness. Her children rise up and call her blessed; Her husband also, and he praises her: "Many daughters have done well, but you excel them all." Charm is deceitful and beauty is passing, but a woman who fears the Lord, she shall be praised. Give her of the fruit of her hands, and let her own works praise her in the gates.

Proverbs 31:10–31

4. ***"Children"*** - Obey parents and live long.

"Children, obey your parents in the Lord, for this is right. 'Honor your father and mother,' which is the first commandment with promise: that it may be well with you and you may live long on the earth" (Ephesians 6:1–3).

VI. God's plan for love and forgiveness:

A. Therefore, as the elect of God, holy and beloved, put on tender mercies, kindness, humility, meekness, longsuffering; bearing with one another, and forgiving one another, if anyone has a complaint against another; even as Christ forgave you, so you also must do. But above all these things put on love, which is the bond of perfection. And let the peace of God rule in your hearts, to which also you were called in one body; and be thankful. Let the word of Christ dwell in you richly in all wisdom, teaching and admonishing one another in psalms and hymns and spiritual songs, singing with grace in your hearts to the Lord. And whatever you do in word or deed, do all in the name of the Lord Jesus, giving thanks to God the Father through Him. Wives, submit to your own husbands, as is fitting in the Lord. Husbands, love your wives and do not be bitter toward them. Children, obey your parents in all things, for this is well pleasing to the Lord. Fathers, do not provoke your children, lest they become discouraged.

Colossians 3:12–21

1. V. 12 - Mercy, kindness, humbleness of mind, and longsuffering.
2. V. 13 - Forgiving one another.
3. V. 14 - Above all things put on LOVE.
4. V. 15 - Let peace rule in your hearts.
5. V. 16 - Let the Word of Christ dwell in you richly.
6. V. 18–19 - Wives submit and Husbands LOVE.

B. Unity through humility:

> Therefore if *there* is any consolation in Christ, if any comfort of love, if any fellowship of the Spirit, if any affection and mercy, fulfill my joy by being like-minded, having the same love, being of one accord, of one mind. *Let* nothing *be done* through selfish ambition or conceit, but in lowliness of mind let each esteem others better than himself. Let each of you look out not only for his own interests, but also for the interests of others. Let this mind be in you which was also in Christ Jesus.
>
> Philippians 2:1–5

1. V. 2 - Be like-minded, in one accord.
2. V. 3 - Esteem each other.
3. V. 4 - Look out for the interest of others.
4. V. 5 - Be Christ-minded.

PART II: COMMUNICATION
Includes Communication Survey

One of the top three problem areas in marriage is "Communication."

I. **Communication:** The exchange of feelings or information, to transfer thought. Involves two people stimulating conversation, one sending and one receiving (correct timing and the choice of words can greatly help our communication).

Communication is the basis for relationship.

A. **Unity and agreement:**
1. No house divided against itself will last or continue to stand.

   "But Jesus knew their thoughts, and said to them: "Every kingdom divided against itself is brought to desolation, and every city or house divided against itself will not stand…" (Matthew 12:25).

2. If two of you agree together about anything, it will come to pass and be done for you by our Father in heaven.

   "Again I say to you that if two of you agree on earth concerning anything that they ask, it will be done for them by My Father in heaven" (Matthew 18:19).

3. Do two walk together, except they make an appointment and have agreed?

"Can two walk together unless they are agreed?" (Amos 3:3).

The power of Unity - There is tremendous power in *UNITY*. However, before Unity can be established, there must first be an agreement between the two people walking together. Nowhere is this principle more true than in the marriage relationship. In order for any marriage to be successful, people have to put aside their own self-centered interests and think of the whole. In effect, they have to die to themselves and be resurrected as brand-new people in Christ who have become *LOVE*-Centered rather than self-centered.

4. "Behold, how good and how pleasant *it is* for brethren to dwell together in unity!" (Psalm 133:1).

5. Bearing with one another and making allowances because you *LOVE* one another. Strive to keep the *harmony* and the *unity* of the Spirit.

   "I, therefore, the prisoner of the Lord, beseech you to walk worthy of the calling with which you were called, with all lowliness and gentleness, with longsuffering, bearing with one another in love, endeavoring to keep the unity of the Spirit in the bond of peace" (Ephesians 4:1–3).

6. Living in harmony, one in purpose:

   "Fulfill my joy by being like-minded, having the same love, *being* of one accord, of one mind" (Philippians 2:2).

7. "*Let* nothing *be done* through selfish ambition or conceit, but in lowliness of mind let each esteem others better than himself. Let each of you look out not only for his own interests, but also for the interests of others. Let this mind be in you which was also in Christ Jesus…" (Philippians 2:3–5).

V. 3 Thinking more highly of one another than you do of yourself.

V. 4 Concerned for the interests of others.

V. 5 Let Jesus be our example.

B. Confession - Words we speak:

1. Let there be no filthiness (e.g., obscenity, indecency) nor foolish and sinful (silly and corrupt) talk, nor coarse jesting, which are not fitting or becoming, but rather giving of "*THANKS.*"

   Therefore be imitators of God as dear children. And walk in love, as Christ also has loved us and given Himself for us, an offering and a sacrifice to God for a sweet-smelling aroma. But fornication and all uncleanness or covetousness, let it not even be named among you, as is fitting for saints; neither filthiness, nor foolish talking, nor coarse jesting, which are not fitting, but rather giving of thanks.

   Ephesians 5:1–4

2. Works of the flesh:

   Now the works of the flesh are evident, which are: adultery, fornication, uncleanness, lewdness, idolatry, sorcery, hatred, contentions, jealousies, outbursts of wrath, selfish ambitions, dissensions, heresies, envy, murders, drunkenness, revelries, and the like; of which I tell you beforehand, just as I also told you in time past, that those who practice such things will not inherit the kingdom of God.

   Galatians 5:19–21

3. Reap what you sow.

   Do not be deceived, God is not mocked; for whatever a man sows, that he will also reap. For he who sows to his flesh will of the flesh reap corruption, but he who sows to the Spirit will of the Spirit reap everlasting life. And let us not grow weary while doing good, for in due season we shall reap if we do not lose heart. Therefore, as we have opportunity, let us do good to all, especially to those who are of the household of faith.

Galatians 6:7–10

4. Order your conversation and conduct aright.

   "Whoever offers praise glorifies Me; And to him who orders *his* conduct *aright* I will show the salvation of God" (Psalm 50:23).

5. Rejecting all falsity, express the *Truth*.

   Therefore, putting away lying, "*Let* each one *of you* speak truth with his neighbor," for we are members of one another. "Be angry, and do not sin:" do not let the sun go down on your wrath, nor give place to the devil. Let him who stole steal no longer, but rather let him labor, working with *his* hands what is good, that he may have something to give him who has need. Let no corrupt word proceed out of your mouth, but what is good for necessary edification, that it may impart grace to the hearers.

   Ephesians 4:25–29

   V. 26–27 When angry, do not sin.

   V. 29 Let no foul or polluting language, nor evil word, nor unwholesome or worthless talk ever come out of your mouth, but only such speech as is good and beneficial.

6. "For he who would love life and see good days, let him refrain his tongue from evil, and his lips from speaking deceit" (1 Peter 3:10).

7. Death and Life are in the power of the tongue.

"A man's stomach shall be satisfied from the fruit of his mouth; From the produce of his lips, he shall be filled. Death and life are in the power of the tongue, and those who love it will eat its fruit" (Proverbs 18:20–21).

C. Be a good listener.

Listening involves paying close attention to what is said and accepting it as another person's thoughts or feelings, right or wrong, without condemnation.

1. Don't answer a matter before you hear the facts.

    "He who answers a matter before he hears *it*, It *is* folly and shame to him" (Proverbs 18:13).

2. Hear counsel, receive instruction, and accept correction.

    "Listen to counsel and receive instruction, that you may be wise in your latter days" (Proverbs 19:20).

3. Be quick to hear (a ready listener), slow to speak, slow to take offense and to get angry. Be good listeners. God gave us two ears and one mouth. Is He telling us something?

    "So then, my beloved brethren, let every man be swift to hear, slow to speak, slow to wrath" (James 1:19).

D. The *Fruit of the Holy Spirit:*

1. The *Fruit of the Holy Spirit* - the work which *His* presence within accomplishes.

Love	*Longsuffering*	*Faithfulness*
Joy	*Kindness*	*Gentleness*
Peace	*Goodness*	*Self-Control*

The *Holy Spirit* removes abrasive qualities from the character of one under *His* control. The *Fruit of the Spirit* knows no season, unlike natural fruit.

    2. "If you abide in Me, and My words abide in you, you will ask what you desire, and it shall be done for you. By this My Father is glorified, that you bear much fruit; so you will be **My disciples**" (John 15:7–8).

    3. You should go and bring forth fruit and that your fruit should remain.

"You did not choose Me, but I chose you and appointed you that you should go and bear fruit, and that your fruit should remain, that whatever you ask the Father in My name He may give you" (John 15:16).

E. Sowing seeds:

    1. "Parable of the Sower"

"The sower sows the word. And these are the ones by the wayside where the word is sown. When they hear, Satan comes immediately and takes away the word that was sown in their hearts. These likewise are the ones sown on stony ground who, when they hear the word, immediately receive it with gladness; and they have no root in themselves, and so endure only for a time. Afterward, when tribulation or persecution arises for the word's sake, immediately they stumble. Now these are the ones sown among thorns; they are the ones who hear the word, and the cares of this world, the deceitfulness of riches, and the desires for other things entering in choke the word, and it becomes unfruitful. But these are the ones sown on good ground, those who hear the word, accept it, and bear fruit: some thirtyfold, some sixty, and some a hundred." Also He said to them, "Is a lamp brought to be put under a basket or under a bed? Is it not to be set on a lampstand?"

Mark 4:14–21

a. V. 20 But these are the ones sown on good ground, those who hear the Word, accept it, and bear fruit: some threefold, some sixty, and some a hundred.

- There are three steps to success in this verse.
★ "Know God's Word" - (hear the Word)
★ "Believe God's Word" - (accept it)
★ "Act on God's Word" - (bear fruit)

b. Every seed produces after its kind.
- What kind of seed are you sowing in your mate?
- What you sow is what you'll harvest.

c. Every seed needs to be tended and nourished.
- Are you caring for the seed you planted?
- Are you watering, feeding, and keeping the weeds out?

d. You will reap a harvest if you don't give up.
- Seeds need time to sprout and grow; don't kill the seed with negative words and not tending them.

e. No farmer plants a seed without expecting a harvest.
- Don't grow weary in well-doing, expect a harvest.

f. The Word is a living seed.
- It can't grow if you don't plant it.

g. Protect each other during dormant, cold times.
- Sometimes we become hard and crusted over, and we need the help of the Holy Spirit to prepare and soften our hearts.

h. Put in the time and effort to maintain your marriage as you did to get your mate.
- Women—helpmate means to continually surround.

i. The Spirit of the Lord gives you the wisdom to tend the fruit.
- Adam tended the garden and dressed it.
- Dress it and make it beautiful.

j. It's never too late to plant a new crop.
- Start today and sow good seeds.
- What you put in is what you'll get out.

k. Never compare your seed with someone else's.
- Don't compare your husband or wife to someone else's.
- Just speak blessings on your mate.

"Now to Him who is able to do exceedingly abundantly above all that we ask or think, according to the power that works in us, **To Him be Glory in the Church and in Christ Jesus throughout all Generations, forever and ever**" (Ephesians 3:20–21).

"Words of Wisdom"

As you wait upon the Lord, you learn to see things from His perspective, move at His pace, and function under His directives. Waiting times are growing times and learning times. As you quiet your heart, you enter His peace; as you sense your weakness, you receive His strength; as you lay down your will, you hear His calling. When you mount up, you are being lifted by the wind of His Spirit... When you move ahead, you are sensitive to His timing... When you act, you give yourself only to the things He has asked you to do.

Ten Commandments of Human Relations

1. Speak to people. There is nothing so nice as a cheerful word of greeting.
2. Smile at people. It takes 72 muscles to frown, only 14 to smile.
3. Call people by name. The sweetest music to anyone's ears is the sound of his/her own name.
4. Be friendly and helpful. If you want friends, you must be one.
5. Be cordial. Speak and act as if everything you do is a joy to you.
6. Be genuinely interested in people. You can like almost everybody, if you try.
7. Be generous with praise and cautious with criticism.
8. Be considerate with the feelings of others. There are usually three sides to controversy: Yours, the other person's, and the right side.
9. Be eager to lend a helping hand. Often it is appreciated more than you know. What counts most in life is what we do for others.
10. Add to this a good sense of humor, a huge dose of patience, and a dash of humility. This combination will open many doors and the rewards will be enormous.

Description of Communication Style

1. Action
   - Focus on: Bottom line, end results, quantity.
   - Strengths: Provide action steps, achieving.
   - Weakness: Insensitive, impatience.

2. Process
   - Focus on: Data/analysis, facts, organization, quality.
   - Strengths: Organized, informed with facts, thorough.
   - Weakness: Hard to please, critical of others, procrastination.

3. People
   - Focus on: People's needs, unity, teamwork, relations.
   - Strengths: Servant, communicator.
   - Weakness: Slow to make decisions, want time.

4. Idea
   - Focus on: New ways, improved, creativity, theories.
   - Strengths: Very visionary, creative.
   - Weakness: Detached, always thinking, planning.

5. Blend
   - Focus on: All of the above, diversity, wide range.
   - Strengths: Easy to approach, diversity.
   - Weakness: Put off, procrastinate.

Questions

Select one of each pair which is most likely to be you. Circle the number and move to the next pair. There are no wrong answers.

1. I like to be doing things.
2. I manage problems in an orderly way.
3. I like change.
4. I think teams are more productive than individuals.
5. I prefer working with people.
6. The future interests me more than the past.
7. I prefer the practical.
8. I enjoy a well-organized meeting.
9. It is best to get things done now.
10. Test new ideas thoroughly before using them.
11. I enjoy trying to think of new possibilities.
12. Interaction with others is a high priority.
13. I can easily take charge in a project.
14. I like to take one thing at a time through to the end.
15. I often stimulate people to think.
41. I enjoy taking on new tasks.
42. The facts speak for themselves.
43. I am in touch with my feelings.
44. I seek to know 'why'.
45. I prefer reading the thoughts of others.
46. I perceive myself as a helper.
47. Do one thing at a time and do it well.
48. Get the job done and do not look back.
49. I inquire about other people's lives.
50. I enjoy doing different things.
51. If you are going to do it, do it right.
52. Be creative and stretch your mind.
53. I am impatient with incompetent people.
54. My mind works fast.
55. Minimize risk by moving slowly.

16. I can often detect what people are feeling.
17. Getting feedback to improve performance is important.
18. A step-by-step approach is best to solve problems.
19. I can sense the emotions beneath the surface.
20. I can find creative solutions.
21. Thinking about the future is enjoyable for me.
22. Meeting other peoples' needs is enjoyable.
23. Success depends on good planning.
24. I am more action than talk.
25. Under pressure I tend to analyze.
26. I learn best through experience.
27. People think I am a good listener.
28. People say I am a creative thinker.
29. I am prone to procrastinate.
30. I am logical and thorough.
31. I am always looking for a better way.
32. I can handle several tasks at the same time.

56. Working cooperatively is more important than working efficiently.
57. I can adjust to circumstances.
58. Feelings are not as trustworthy as facts
59. Being liked is important to me.
60. I usually grasp an idea very quickly.
61. People think I am a visionary.
62. People say I am good with details
63. I prefer productivity/ accomplishment.
64. Good relationships are essential.
65. I am quick to take on a new job.
66. I take the initiative to make new people feel comfortable.
67. I often think about the purpose of life.
68. Getting things done is my strength.
69. Organizing is one of my strengths.
70. Getting things done is my strength.
71. Finding meaning is important to me.
72. Working together is better than just working.

33. I can make quick decisions.

34. I follow my head more than my heart.

35. I like seeing the bigger picture.

36. It is best to talk out your problems.

37. Thinking should always proceed action.

38. I am good at encouraging others.

39. I accomplish more by working alone.

40. I like to start things and let others finish them.

73. I play with ideas even if they are impractical.

74. I believe rules are made to be followed.

75. Quality is to be preferred over quantity.

76. I learn better in groups.

77. I make decisions in a methodical way.

78. I like ideals and tend to be idealistic.

79. I say what I mean and man what I say.

80. I am very accepting of others.

Type of Communicator

How did you score? Circle the same number you circled on the question sheet.

1. Action
   1-7-9-13-17-24-26-32-33-39-41-48-50-53-57-63-65-70-74-79
2. Process
   2-8-10-14-18-23-25-30-34-37-42-47-51-55-58-62-66-69-75-77
3. People
   4-5-12-16-19-22-27-29-36-38-43-46-49-56-59-64-68-72-76-80
4. Idea
   3-6-11-15-20-21-28-31-35-40-44-45-52-54-60-61-67-71-73-78

Count the number of circles in each one and write the number in front of each type in space provided.

– Your highest score is the one you are most comfortable with and committed to.
– Your lowest score is the one you are least comfortable with and in using it.
– You may use one of the four at different times, as the circumstances may call for.
– If you are under pressure or stress you usually revert to your highest communicator style.
– If you are one to four points of all four, you are a BLEND.

Description of Communication Style

1. Action
   - Focus on: Bottom line, end results, quantity.
   - Strengths: Provide action steps, achieving.
   - Weakness: Insensitive, impatience.

2. Process
   - Focus on: Data/analysis, facts, organization, quality.
   - Strengths: Organized, informed with facts, thorough.
   - Weakness: Hard to please, critical of others, procrastination.

3. People
   - Focus on: People's needs, unity, teamwork, relations.
   - Strengths: Servant, communicator.
   - Weakness: Slow to make decisions, want time.

4. Idea
   - Focus on: New ways, improved, creativity, theories.
   - Strengths: Very visionary, creative.
   - Weakness: Be detached, always thinking, planning.

5. Blend
   - Focus on: All of above, diversity, wide range.
   - Strengths: Easy to approach, diversity.
   - Weakness: Put off, procrastinate.

Part III: Money
Includes Financial Management Survey

One of the top three problem areas in marriage is "Money."
Money—wealth; representing gold or silver; any medium of exchange, especially as issued by a government or authorized public authority. In the USA we call our money the "dollar." Other forms of exchange are checks, bonds, certificates, and so forth.

A. Whose *Money?*

1. Regardless of who makes the most money, it is essential that you operate in the "**OUR MONEY**" frame of mind, not "MY MONEY' and "YOUR MONEY." There are choices about money to be made nearly every day. When you are married, those choices need to be made together because this is a joint venture, not two corporations doing business under one roof.

2. This is not always an easy adjustment to make since you may have been accustomed to making decisions about money on your own and probably feel you are pretty good at it. You must now consider the feelings and thoughts of your "other half" as you make these decisions. This could be difficult unless you make the effort to communicate well.

3. To promote the best communication and teamwork skills, we encourage both of you to spend time together each month reviewing your BUDGET or financial

matters. Don't let the responsibility for your finances fall on just one person/spouse. Instead, discuss your spending habits and the outstanding bills you have to pay. Pray about your needs/desires and ask God to lead you in setting goals that both of you agree on. Resolve to let "Money Management" forge a deeper unity in your marriage rather than drive a wedge between you.

"Again I say to you that if two of you agree on earth concerning anything that they ask, it will be done for them by My Father in heaven" (Matthew 18:19).

4. Although both of you should know how to balance your checkbook, read your bank statement, pay bills, and handle the details, we suggest that only one person (at a time) keep the books. If you want, you can rotate these responsibilities every six months or so, but two people usually cannot simultaneously keep the records. Unless you assign different areas of responsibility in your record keeping and paying of bills.

B. Being opposites can be a positive.

1. In His wisdom, God made opposites to attract. Being attracted to opposite qualities in each other can have many benefits. Imagine how awkward it would be if both of you had no sense of direction, but if one of you has this quality, at least you will know where you are.

2. Having opposite personality characteristics can be an asset in handling money as well. One person will have a bent toward budgeting and saving; the other will lean toward spending and borrowing. The amount of leaning in either direction will depend upon the individual personality and influence.

C. **"Overspending" or "Hoarding": Discovering your tendencies in Money Management.**
   1. Money represents economic power that can be abused in at least two ways: Hoarding or Overspending. Most people have the tendency to lean in one direction or the other. However, some are more balanced.
   2. Hoarding takes responsible saving to the extreme by accumulating far above and beyond what is required for basic needs. Legitimate family needs may be overlooked or neglected when a person has this tendency. This type of individual sometimes is described as tight, stingy, frugal, cheap, or miserly.
   3. As you might imagine, the marriage of a hoarder to an overspender could set the stage for marital stress. Left unresolved, this stress also could become a wedge used by satan to cause division between husband and wife.

D. **Characteristics of an Overspender:**
   1. Quite often overspenders don't have well-defined goals. As a result they seldom have a clear plan of action for financial management or budgeting. Instead, they seem to be more spontaneous or impulsive. As a result, the life of an overspender is often chaotic and is marked by a series of financial emergencies and gleeful purchases. This is often characterized by people who habitually shuffle more money than they have through their accounts. The inability to say "no" to the latest new electronic gadget, toy, or sale at the mall makes the overspender easy prey in today's world of advertising and easy credit. Usually the overspender will misuse credit cards.
   2. Often overspenders are too optimistic in projecting how far their money will go. They think in terms of

how much the payment for something will be rather than counting the whole cost in light of established financial goals.

3. However, this can be a positive situation if each marriage partner realizes his or her strengths and weaknesses in handling money.

4. There are a number of spiritual issues that can give rise to a lifestyle of overspending. The scripture passages listed below show you what God's Word says about the spiritual dimension of overspending. Overspending could affect giving.

   a. Greed, sensual desires:

   "What leads to [the unending] quarrels and conflicts among you? Do they not come from your [hedonistic] desires that war in your [bodily] members [fighting for control over you]?" (James 4:1, AMP).

   b. Lack of self-control:

   "Whoever has no rule over his own spirit Is like a city broken down, without walls" (Proverbs 25:28).

   c. Command those who are rich in this present age not to be haughty, nor to trust in uncertain riches but in the living God, who gives us richly all things to enjoy. Let them do good, that they be rich in good works, ready to give, willing to share, storing up for themselves a good foundation for the time to come, that they may lay hold on eternal life.

   1 Timothy 6:17–19

   V. 17 Pride.

   V. 18 Be ready to share (AMP).

d. Lack of faith

Do not fret because of evildoers, nor be envious of the workers of iniquity. For they shall soon be cut down like the grass, and wither as the green herb. Trust in the Lord, and do good; dwell in the land, and feed on His faithfulness. Delight yourself also in the Lord, and He shall give you the desires of your heart. Commit your way to the Lord, trust also in Him, and He shall bring it to pass. He shall bring forth your righteousness as the light, and your justice as the noonday.

Psalm 37:1–6

V. 3 Trust in the Lord.

V. 4 Delight yourself in the Lord.

V. 5 Commit your way to the Lord.

e. Lust of the flesh, and lust of the eye, and pride of life:

Do not love the world or the things in the world. If anyone loves the world, the love of the Father is not in him. For all that is in the world--the lust of the flesh, the lust of the eyes, and the pride of life--is not of the Father but is of the world. And the world is passing away, and the lust of it; but he who does the will of God abides forever.

1 John 2:15–17

V. 16 "Lust of the flesh, and lust of the eye, and pride of life."

1. Adam and Eve tempted in the same three areas.

"So when the woman saw that the tree was good for food, that it was pleasant to the eyes, and a tree desirable to make one wise, she took of its fruit and ate. She also gave to her husband with her, and he ate" (Genesis 3:6).

2. Jesus temped by satan in all three areas.

But He answered and said, "It is written, 'Man shall not live by bread alone, but by every word that proceeds from the mouth of God.' Then the devil took Him up into the holy city, set Him on the pinnacle of the temple, and said to Him, "If You are the Son of God, throw Yourself down. For it is written: 'He shall give His angels charge over you,' and, 'In their hands they shall bear you up, Lest you dash your foot against a stone.'" Jesus said to him, "It is written again, 'You shall not tempt the Lord your God.'" Again, the devil took Him up on an exceedingly high mountain and showed Him all the kingdoms of the world and their glory. And he said to Him, "All these things I will give You if You will fall down and worship me." Then Jesus said to him, "Away with you, Satan! For it is written, 'You shall worship the Lord your God, and Him only you shall serve.'"

Matthew 4:4–10

Then Jesus, being filled with the Holy Spirit, returned from the Jordan and was led by the Spirit into the wilderness, being tempted for forty days by the devil. And in those days He ate nothing, and afterward, when they had ended, He was hungry. And the devil said to Him, "If You are the Son of God, command this stone to become bread." But Jesus answered him, saying, "It is written, 'Man shall not live by bread alone, but by every word of God.'" Then the devil, taking Him up on a high mountain, showed Him all the kingdoms of the world in a moment of time. And the devil said to Him, "All this authority I will give You, and their glory; for this has been delivered to me, and I give it to whomever I wish. Therefore, if You will worship before me, all will be Yours."

And Jesus answered and said to him, "Get behind Me, Satan! For it is written, 'You shall worship the Lord your God, and Him only you shall serve.'" Then he brought Him to Jerusalem, set Him on the pinnacle of the temple, and said to Him, "If You are the Son of God, throw Yourself down from here. For it is written: 'He shall give His angels charge over you, To keep you,' and, 'In their hands they shall bear you up, Lest you dash your foot against a stone.'" And Jesus answered and said to him, "It has been said, 'You shall not tempt the Lord your God.'" Now when the devil had ended every temptation, he departed from Him until an opportune time.

Luke 4:1–13

3. Both Adam and Jesus faced three aspects of temptation. Adam yielded, bringing upon humankind sin and death. Jesus resisted, resulting in "*Justification*" and "*Life*."

f. Lack of contentment:

   If anyone teaches otherwise and does not consent to wholesome words, even the words of our Lord Jesus Christ, and to the doctrine which accords with godliness, he is proud, knowing nothing, but is obsessed with disputes and arguments over words, from which come envy, strife, reviling, evil suspicions, useless wranglings of men of corrupt minds and destitute of the truth, who suppose that godliness is a means of gain. From such withdraw yourself. Now godliness with contentment is great gain. For we brought nothing into this world, and it is certain we can carry nothing out. And having food and clothing, with these we shall be content."

1 Timothy 6:3–8

V. 7 "We brought nothing into this world, and it is certain we can carry nothing out."

E. Characteristics of a hoarder:

Hoarders are just as compulsive about saving as spenders are about spending. You can see how being married to someone of the opposite extreme is a prescription for ongoing marital conflict. Because hoarders often are driven by a fear of not having enough money, they try to hang onto every penny. Frequently they have an unrealistic financial plan of setting aside as much money as possible, which may result in the neglect of daily needs. Finding the absolute best bargain on an item before purchasing it may become an obsession. Like the overspender, a number of spiritual issues can feed a lifestyle of hoarding. Below are scripture passages to discover what God's Word says about the spiritual dimensions of hoarding. A hoarder could tend to have trouble in giving and helping people.

1. Fear:

Therefore I say to you, do not worry about your life, what you will eat or what you will drink; nor about your body, what you will put on. Is not life more than food and the body more than clothing? Look at the birds of the air, for they neither sow nor reap nor gather into barns; yet your heavenly Father feeds them. Are you not of more value than they? Which of you by worrying can add one cubit to his stature? So why do you worry about clothing? Consider the lilies of the field, how they grow: they neither toil nor spin; and yet I say to you that even Solomon in all his glory was not arrayed like one of these. Now if God so clothes the grass of the field, which today is, and tomorrow is thrown into the oven, will He not much more clothe you, O you of little faith? Therefore, do not worry, saying, "What shall we eat?" or "What shall we drink?" or "What shall we wear?" For after all these things the Gentiles seek. For your heavenly Father knows that you need all these things. But seek first the kingdom of God and His righteousness, and all these things shall be added to you. Therefore, do not worry about tomorrow, for tomorrow will worry about its own things. Sufficient for the day is its own trouble.

Matthew 6:25–34

- V. 25 "Do not be worried about your life, what you shall eat or what you shall drink, or about your body, what you shall put in it."
- V. 31 "Do not worry."

2. Pride:

And He said to them, "Take heed and beware of covetousness, for one's life does not consist in the abundance of the things he possesses." Then He spoke a parable to them, saying: "The ground of a certain rich man yielded plentifully. And he thought within himself, saying, 'What shall I do, since I have no room to store my crops?' So he said, 'I will do this: I will pull down my barns and build greater, and there I will store all my crops and my goods. And I will say to my soul, "Soul, you have many goods laid up for many years; take your ease; eat, drink, and be merry."' But God said to him, "Fool! This night your soul will be required of you; then whose will those things be which you have provided?" So is he who lays up treasure for himself, and is not rich toward God.

Luke 12:15–21

V. 15 Take heed and beware of covetousness, for one's life does not consist in the abundance of the things he possesses.

3. Without faith, it is impossible to please God.

"But without faith it is impossible to please Him, for he who comes to God must believe that He is, and that He is a rewarder of those who diligently seek Him" (Hebrews 11:6).

4. "Let there be no sexual immorality, impurity, or greed among you. Such sins have no place among God's people" (Ephesians 5:3, NLT).

V. 3 "Greediness must not even be named among you" (AMP).

5. Love God, not money. Use money for God's glory.

But those who desire to be rich fall into temptation and a snare, and into many foolish and harmful lusts which drown men in destruction and perdition. For the love of money is a root of all kinds of evil, for which some have strayed from the faith in their greediness, and pierced themselves through with many sorrows.

1 Timothy 6:9–10

F. Learning to work as a Team

You and your spouse probably bring many differences into your marriage. Some differences may be due to the family you grew up in, or the natural gender differences between a male and female, the different socioeconomic backgrounds, and the different education experiences. In fact, you may have become alarmed about how different the two of you really are.

Not to worry. One of the mysteries of marriage is how beautifully God can weave two different lives into one pattern of unity that reflects His glory. There are two critical dimensions to achieving this unity: a *"spiritual"* dimension and a *"practical."* Both of these dimensions need prayer and discussion time together. The *first step* toward building teamwork and unity in your marriage is to honor a clear commitment to the Lord Jesus Christ. Only He can free you from bondage to selfish desires and wants. Only Jesus can enable you to fully love one another and to cherish each other. And even though you cannot make another person love you, you can live your life under the Lordship of Jesus Christ. The *second step* in learning to work as a team is to commit to live by a budget. A planned approach to govern your future spending can bring balance and compromise to your money management. If you do not live on a budget, you probably are not handling your finances properly. Don't minimize the importance of getting your financial act together through the use of a budget.

Write the vision down.

"Then the Lord answered me and said: "Write the vision and make it plain on tablets, That he may run who reads it" (Habakkuk 2:2).

God wants us to be good stewards with the money and possessions He brings into our lives.

Common Budgeting Myths

Myth: We have tried a budget once and it didn't work.

Truth: New skills are not perfected on the first try. If you have tried budgeting previously, you are in the best position to succeed, because you can benefit from your previous mistakes and experiences. You know it takes effort and you can be determined to make a lasting change.

Myth: We live on a variable income and, therefore, cannot budget.

Truth: More than anyone, people on variable incomes should budget. Although your income varies, you still need to follow a budget to ensure that your expenses do not exceed your average variable income.

Myth: We don't earn enough income to budget.

Truth: You definitely need a budget. The smaller your income, the stronger your need for a budget. When you budget, you limit excess spending, and it's as if your income grows.

Myth: We earn too much income to worry about a budget.

Truth: Although you may be blessed with an above average income, a budget can help you be a good steward with your surplus. Unfortunately, as incomes rise, the expenses rise at the same or a greater rate. Setting a plan and keeping a budget will help you use your growing income for the benefit of your family and others.

Myth: We don't have time to keep track of a budget.

Truth: It takes far more time to handle a financial mess than it does to keep your finances in order. Remember, "An ounce of prevention is worth a pound of cure." Keeping a budget takes less time than you think.⁸

The Purpose of a Budget

To help you plan to live within your means as a good steward.

What a Budget Does

1. Helps you determine the difference between:
   - Needs
   - Wants
   - Desires
2. Helps you find problem areas.

What a Budget Won't Do

Automatically relieve your indebtedness.

Start living on a budget and get on the road to financial freedom.

Estimated Monthly Budget
(Monthly Income and Expenses)

GROSS MONTHLY INCOME
Salary _____
Interest _____
Dividends _____
Other Income _____

LESS
1. Tithe/Giving _____
2. Taxes (Fed, State, FICA) _____

NET SPENDABLE INCOME _____
===============

LIVING EXPENSES
3. Housing
   Mortgage/Rent _____
   Insurance _____
   Property Taxes _____
   Electricity _____
   Gas _____
   Water _____
   Sanitation _____
   Telephone _____
   Maintenance _____
   Cable TV _____
   Internet _____
   Other _____
4. Food _____
5. Transportation _____
   Payments _____
   Gas and Oil _____
   Insurance _____
   License/Taxes _____
   Maintenance/Repair/Replace _____
   Other _____
6. Insurance
   Life _____
   Health _____
   Other _____
7. Debts _____

8. Entertainment/Recreation _____
   Eating Out _____
   Babysitters _____
   Activities/Trips _____
   Vacation _____
   Pets _____
   Other _____
9. Clothing _____
10. Savings _____
11. Medical Expenses _____
    Doctor _____
    Dentist _____
    Prescriptions _____
    Other _____
12. Miscellaneous _____
    Toilitries/Cosmetics _____
    Beauty/Barber _____
    Laundry/Cleaning _____
    Allowances _____
    Subscriptions _____
    Gifts (incl Christmas) _____
    Cash _____
    Other _____
13. School/Child Care _____
    Tuition _____
    Materials _____
    Transportation _____
    Day Care _____
13. Investments _____

TOTAL LIVING EXPENSES _____

INCOME VS. LIVING EXPENSES:
Net Spendable Income _____
Less Total Living Expenses _____
Surplus or Deficit _____

"God's Plan for Marriage and the Family"
"Money" Part II

Financial Management Survey – Discover your tendencies.

Instructions – Mark an __X__ by the statement that is closest to your situation. Mark either the numbered or lettered question in each case. Mark the numbered statement on the left and the lettered statement on the right.

	Number	Letter	
1.	_____	_____	I set aside savings from each paycheck.
A.	_____	_____	Since it takes all I can make to live on, I don't have any savings.
2.	_____	_____	I don't use a credit card or, if I do, I pay the balance in full each month.
A.	_____	_____	I usually carry over a balance on my credit cards each month.
3.	_____	_____	I know exactly how my money is spent.
A.	_____	_____	I have a hard time figuring out where all my money goes.
4.	_____	_____	I pay all my bills on time.
A.	_____	_____	I am sometimes late in paying my bills.
5.	_____	_____	I usually put off buying something in order to think about it for a while.
A.	_____	_____	When I see something I really want, I usually buy it.

6. _____ _____ I have money set aside for paying taxes, repairing the car, or other needs.

A. _____ _____ I usually have to charge (borrow) to cover unexpected expenditures and then make payments to pay it off.

7. _____ _____ I never borrow money except to buy a house or a car.

A. _____ _____ I sometimes borrow money from friends or relatives to get by.

8. _____ _____ I follow a systematic plan for saving money.

A. _____ _____ It takes all I earn to afford my curreent standard of living.

9. _____ _____ I balance my checkbook with my monthly bank statement without any major problems.

A. _____ _____ I have difficulty balancing my checkbook.

10. _____ _____ I am very careful to control my spending.

A. _____ _____ If I have money available, I usually have something already selected to spend it on.

11. _____ _____ I live on a budget.

A. _____ _____ I don't make enough money (or I make too much money) to worry about budgeting.

12. _____ _____ I try not to buy unnecessary items if I can help it.

A. _____ _____ I tend to buy things I don't really need.

13. _____ _____ My family and friends would say that I am a saver.

A. _____ _____ My family and friends would say that I am a spender.

14. _____ _____ I believe most people would get by if they would learn to live on what they make.

A. _____ _____ If I just made more money, theen I could get by.

15. _____ _____ It makes me feel good to save money.

A. _____ _____ It makes me feel good to buy something new.

16. _____ _____ I save before I spend.

A. _____ _____ I save what I have left over after I spend it.

17. _____ _____ I save money because money provides security.

A. _____ _____ I plan to start a savings program when I get better off financially.

18. _____ _____ It's very important for me to have money.

A. _____ _____ I could care less about having a lot of money.

19. _____ _____ It's more important to save money.

A. _____ _____ It's more important for me to live comfortably.

20. _____ _____ I never write checks unless I have sufficient funds in my account.

A. _____ _____ I sometimes pay a charge for overdrawing my checking account.

21. _____ _____ Staying out of deebt is more important to me.

A. _____ _____ Having a new car, lots of clothes, a nice house is more important to me.

22. _____ _____ It's really more like me to be stingy with my money.

A. _____ _____ It's really more like me to be generous with my money.

23. _____ _____ I would rather live in a shack and wear used clothes than have debts.

A. _____ _____ I have some debts, but that is normal in today's society.

24. _____ _____ I have a strong desire to be wealthy.

A. _____ _____ I don't worry about how much money I have.

25. _____ _____ I believe people have to accumulate wealth to live successfully.

A. _____ _____ I like to have nice things, but I could care less about accumulating money.

26. _____ _____ It's more important to save money than have nice things.

A. _____ _____ Having nice clothes and driving a new car are part of my lifestyle.

27. _____ _____			As a young person I had my own savings account and regularly put aside money from my own earnings.
A. _____ _____			I usually spent my earnings and was not able to save any.
28. _____ _____			When I graduated from high school and started college, I had some of my own money set aside for my education.
A. _____ _____			I had no money set aside from my personal earnings when I graduated.
29. _____ _____			As a young person, I was generally frugal with my money and usually had some stashed away for things I really needed.
A. _____ _____			As a young person, I was pretty carefree with my money and never seemed to have enough.
30. _____ _____			While growing up, I generally avoided the fads and stuck to the basics.
A. _____ _____			While growing up, I purchased a lot of things that were fads and later realized I really didn't need them.
31. _____ _____			You don't like to give money to help people.
A. _____ _____			You like helping people with food, clothing, and sometimes with money.
32. _____ _____			You don't like to spend money on your family.

A. _____	_____	You like buying things for your family.
33. _____	_____	You have difficulty giving to others and to good causes.
A. _____	_____	You enjoy giving, and especially to God's work.

Scoring your survey;

Your answers to the survey are arranged to fall into two columns: Left and Right. Each of you total your responses in each column and record your totals below. Then subtract the total of the Right column from the total in the Left column. (Note: you may end up with a negative number). Then plot your number on the scale below.

	Score X	**Example**
Total responses, left column (number)	_____	_____
Total responses, right column (number)	_____	_____
Grand Total:	_____	_____

Now plot your net totals on the scale below

Overspender	-	Spender	Balanced	Saver	-	Hoarder
-25	-15	-5	0	5	15	25

Part IV: Sex in Marriage

One of the top three problem areas in marriage is "Sex."

A. **Marriage God's way:**

1. It is not good for man to be alone: I will make a helper suitable for him.

    "And the Lord God said, 'It is not good that man should be alone; I will make him a helper comparable to him'" (Genesis 2:18).

2. So God created man in His own image; in the image of God He created him; male and female He created them. Then God blessed them, and God said to them, "Be fruitful and multiply; fill the earth and subdue it; have dominion over the fish of the sea, over the birds of the air, and over every living thing that moves on the earth."

    Genesis 1:27–28

    > V. 28 **"*Be fruitful*" and "*Multiply*":** fill the earth and subdue it: have dominion over the Earth.

3. God has always intended the sex relationship to be far more than just an act. It is not gland calling out to gland, but a husband expressing total devotion to his wife who has given her life into his hands and trusts him fully with her body and her heart.

    "Wives, submit to your own husbands, as is fitting in the Lord. Husbands, love your wives and do not be bitter toward them" (Colossians 3:18–19).

B. **Good rules to follow concerning sex:**
1. Sex is exclusively designed for a husband and wife, completely alone with each other.

    a. "Therefore a man[woman] shall leave his[her] father and mother and be joined to his[her] wife[husband], and they shall become one flesh. And they were both naked, the man and his wife, and were not ashamed" (Genesis 2:24–25).

    b. "Marriage is honorable among all, and the bed undefiled; but fornicators and adulterers God will judge" (Hebrews 13:4).

2. No sexual act should be entered into if it offends either spouse.

    Wives, submit to your own husbands, as to the Lord. For the husband is head of the wife, as also Christ is head of the church; and He is the Savior of the body. Therefore, just as the church is subject to Christ, so let the wives be to their own husbands in everything. Husbands, love your wives, just as Christ also loved the church and gave Himself for her.

    Ephesians 5:22–25

3. Sex should be an act of giving and not of forcing.

    "Let nothing be done through selfish ambition or conceit, but in lowliness of mind let each esteem others better than himself. Let each of you look out not only for his own interests, but also for the interests of others (Philippians 2:3–4).

4. Husband and wife responsibility concerning intimacy.

    Now concerning the things of which you wrote to me: It is good for a man not to touch a woman. Nevertheless, because of sexual immorality, let each man have his own wife, and let each woman have her own husband. Let the husband render to his wife the affection due her, and likewise also the wife to her husband. The wife does not have authority over her own body, but the husband does. And likewise the husband does not have authority over his own body, but the wife does. Do not deprive one another except with consent for a time, that you may give yourselves to fasting and prayer; and come together again so that Satan does not tempt you because of your lack of self-control.

1 Corinthians 7:1–5

5. "Let your fountain be blessed, and rejoice with the wife of your youth. As a loving deer and a graceful doe, let her breasts satisfy you at all times; and always be enraptured with her love" (Proverbs 5:18–19).

C. The "role" of sex in marriage:

1. Sex strengthens the bond between husband and wife. A satisfying sexual relationship helps to keep a couple together and close.

2. Sex fosters the growth of intimacy (a special type of friendship) in the relationship.

3. Sex helps to provide a special privateness that excludes all others from the relationship.

4. Sex overcomes many conflicts and helps a couple to come back together whenever there is a rift.

5. Sex serves to reduce stress and anxiety by providing a special time of togetherness and release of tension.

6. Sex can become a wonderful way of expressing love between a couple.

7. The pleasure of sex provides a shared experience, even when not much else is shared in common in a relationship.
8. Sex provides a special sense of emotional security that helps to create a sense of well-being and happiness.

These are all positive benefits that help to strengthen a marriage. But is everything about sex positive? No, it isn't. Sometimes sex or the withholding of it is used to punish a partner. Sexual frustration can cause a great deal of hostility in an unfulfilled partner. And when sex is used to express hostility or to manipulate a partner, it has stopped being beneficial. It may even be destructive. Essential to a satisfactory sexual relationship is an atmosphere of mutual caring, friendliness, openness, sharing of feelings, and commitment. There must be mutual tolerance for shortcomings, a spirit of forgiveness, mutual concern, trust, and freedom from fear. In short, there must be **"LOVE."**

D. Seven major differences between most "men" and "women":

	Women	Men
1.	Emotional (deeply caring)	Chauvinistic (cold logic)
2.	Relationship oriented	Work oriented
3.	Enjoy the process	Enjoy reaching a goal
4.	Know by intuition	Know by analyzing
5.	Physically weaker	Physically stronger
6.	Often feel depressed	Often feel inadequate
7.	Focused on the present and past simultaneously	Focused on the present or present and future

Men aren't always right. Women aren't always right. The battle of the sexes can only rightly end in *acting* upon the **"Word of God,"** because God is always right.

E. **Points of wisdom:**

1. "Therefore whoever hears these **sayings of Mine**, and does them, I will liken him to a wise man who built his house on the rock" (Matthew 7:24).

2. Discuss with your spouse the difference between romance and sex. List some of the most romantic things you did when you were courting. If possible, try these activities again. Enjoy the results.

3. When we do what we can, God will do what we can't!

"For with God nothing will be impossible" (Luke 1:37).

F. **Common sense comments:**

1. Make Christ the head of your home; husband and wife both strive to please Jesus and you'll be at peace with each other.

2. Don't hurt the one God has put by your side.

3. Keep first Love; never forget or stop saying the little things you did or said when you first fell in Love.

4. Let your children see father and mother hugging and showing Love to each other, showing affection one to another.

5. Husband and wife communicate with each other; don't take for granted the other knows.

6. Do little things for each other, no matter how small. Sometimes it's the little things that mean the most.

7. Women, you are not to be ahead or behind your husband, but by his side. After all, you came from man's side.
8. Husband and wife, don't keep track of wrongdoings. Jesus is our example. He said, Father, forgive them for they know not what they do.
9. What you put into your marriage is what you will get out. What kind of seed are you sowing into each other's lives?
10. Don't compare your mate with someone else.
11. Always keep regular dates, just the two of you, so you can share and stay close to each other.
12. Don't embarrass your spouse in public.

G. The Beatitudes for Married Couples

- BLESSED are the husbands and wives who continue to be affectionate, considerate, and courteous long after the wedding bells have ceased ringing.

- BLESSED are they who have a sense of humor and laugh together, for this will be a handy shock absorber.

- BLESSED are they who Love their mates more than any other person, who joyfully remain faithful to one another, and continue to build for their family.

- BLESSED are they who remember to thank God for their food and who take time daily to read the Bible and pray.

- BLESSED are mates who never speak loudly or disrespectfully to one another and who make their home a place "where seldom is heard a discouraging word."

- BLESSED are the husband and wife who regularly worship in their church and who work together for the advancement of Christ's Kingdom.

- BLESSED are they who arrive at a satisfactory mature understanding concerning financial matters.

- BLESSED are the husband and wife who humbly dedicate their lives and their home to Christ and who practice the teachings of Christ in the home.

Part V: Parents' Responsibility for Children

I. Let's look at the "Family" - according to "God's Word."
   A. **Children are a gift from God.**
   "Behold, children are a heritage from the Lord, the fruit of the womb is a reward" (Psalm 127:3).
   B. **Train up a child.**
   "Train up a child in the way he should go, and when he is old he will not depart from it" (Proverbs 22:6).
   C. **Give discipline and correction.**
      1. Discipline right away:
      "Because the sentence against an evil work is not executed speedily, therefore the heart of the sons of men is fully set in them to do evil" (Ecclesiastes 8:11).
         a. Love and correction:
         "For whom the Lord loves He corrects, just as a father the son in whom he delights" (Proverbs 3:12).
      2. Correction or Hell:
      "Do not withhold correction from a child, for if you beat him with a rod, he will not die. You shall

beat him with a rod and deliver his soul from hell" (Proverbs 23:13–14).

3. Foolishness or correction:

   "Foolishness is bound up in the heart of a child; the rod of correction will drive it far from him" (Proverbs 22:15).

4. Did not correct:

   "For I have told him that I will judge his house forever for the iniquity which he knows, because his sons made themselves vile, and he did not restrain them" (1 Samuel 3:13).

5. "A foolish son is a grief to his father, and bitterness to her who bore him" (Proverbs 17:25).

6. Spare not for his crying:

   "A brother offended is harder to win than a strong city, and contentions are like the bars of a castle" (Proverbs 18:19).

7. Rod for the back of him:

   "Wisdom is found on the lips of him who has understanding, but a rod is for the back of him who is devoid of understanding" (Proverbs 10:13).

8. Reproof and wisdom (or shame):

   "The rod and rebuke give wisdom, but a child left to himself brings shame to his mother. Correct your son, and he will give you rest; yes, he will give delight to your soul" (Proverbs 29:15, 17).

9. Sparing the rod:

   "He who spares his rod hates his son, but he who **loves him** disciplines him promptly" (Proverbs 13:24).

10. Fruit of righteousness:

"Now no chastening seems to be joyful for the present, but painful; nevertheless, afterward it yields the peaceable fruit of righteousness to those who have been trained by it" (Hebrews 12:11).

D. Instruction and training:

1a. Father gives instructions.

"A wise son heeds his father's instruction, but a scoffer does not listen to rebuke" (Proverbs 13:1).

1b. Instructions from father.

Hear, my children, the instruction of a father, And give attention to know understanding; For I give you good doctrine: Do not forsake my law. When I was my father's son, tender and the only one in the sight of my mother, He also taught me, and said to me: "Let your heart retain my words; keep my commands, and live.

Proverbs 4:1–4

2. Father shall make known God's **"Truth."**

"The living, the living man, he shall praise You, as I do this day; the father shall make known Your truth to the children" (Isaiah 38:19).

3. Teach young men and women.

"That they admonish the young women to love their husbands, to love their children, to be discreet, chaste, homemakers, good, obedient to their own husbands, that the word of God may not be blasphemed. Likewise exhort the young men to be sober-minded" (Titus 2:4–6).

4. Provoke not, but love, nurture, train, discipline, teach, and advise your children.

"And you, fathers, do not provoke your children to wrath, but bring them up in the training and admonition of the Lord" (Ephesians 6:4).

5. Teach God's commands to your children.

Hear, O Israel: The Lord our God, the Lord is one! You shall love the Lord your God with all your heart, with all your soul, and with all your strength. "And these words which I command you today shall be in your heart. You shall teach them diligently to your children, and shall talk of them when you sit in your house, when you walk by the way, when you lie down, and when you rise up. You shall bind them as a sign on your hand, and they shall be as frontlets between your eyes. You shall write them on the doorposts of your house and on your gates.

Deuteronomy 6:4–9

E. **Teach children to work—**

1a. Six days work; seventh day, you shall do no work:

Six days you shall labor and do all your work, but the seventh day is the Sabbath of the Lord your God. In it you shall do no work: you, nor your son, nor your daughter, nor your male servant, nor your female servant, nor your cattle, nor your stranger who is within your gates.

Exodus 20:9–10

1b. Begin using your hands for honest work:

Let him who stole steal no longer, but rather let him labor, working with his hands what is good, that he may have something to give him who has need.

Ephesians 4:28

F. **Parents, be the right example:**
   1. Showing thyself a pattern.

      In all things showing yourself to be a pattern of good works; in doctrine showing integrity, reverence, incorruptibility, sound speech that cannot be condemned, that one who is an opponent may be ashamed, having nothing evil to say of you. Exhort bondservants to be obedient to their own masters, to be well pleasing in all things, not answering back.

      Titus 2:7–9

   2. Be a good example.

      "Imitate me, just as I also imitate Christ" (1 Corinthians 11:1).

   3. Timothy's mother and grandmother were good examples.

      "When I call to remembrance the genuine faith that is in you, which dwelt first in your grandmother Lois and your mother Eunice, and I am persuaded is in you also" (2 Timothy 1:5).

G. **Unity and Agreement in the Family:**
   1. A house divided shall not stand.

      "But Jesus knew their thoughts and said to them: "Every kingdom divided against itself is brought to desolation, and every city or house divided against itself will not stand" (Matthew 12:25).

   2. Agreement is powerful.

      "Again I say to you that if two of you agree on earth concerning anything that they ask, it will be done for them by My Father in heaven" (Matthew 18:19).

H. **Wisdom, Truth, and Joy**
   1. A wise child brings joy.

      "The father of the righteous will greatly rejoice, and he who begets a wise child will delight in him. Let your father and your mother be glad and let her who bore you rejoice" (Proverbs 23:24–25).

   2. Joy and truth.

      "I have no greater joy than to hear that my children walk in truth" (3 John 1:4).

   3. Even Jesus was subject to His parents and increased in **WISDOM, STATURE,** and in **FAVOR** with God and man.

      "Then He went down with them and came to Nazareth, and was subject to them, but His mother kept all these things in her heart. And Jesus increased in wisdom and stature, and in favor with God and men" (Luke 2:51–52).

Common Sense Comments

1. Father or Mother - you can teach your children to love and respect their father or mother by the way you talk about your mate in front of your children, whether your mate is there or not.
2. With children - say what you mean and mean what you say.
3. Consistency is very important. Be consistent on follow through, not "OKAY" one day and "NO" the next.
4. Don't lie to your children; always tell the truth. Example: where they come from (birth); Easter bunny vs. the Resurrection of Christ; Santa Claus vs. Jesus, and so forth.
5. Have set rules - Father and Mother agree on and stick to them. Children need guidelines.
6. Father or Mother never interfere with the other when correcting a Child. If you disagree, talk it over later in private—even with a blended family.
7. Never allow children to have rebellion, back talk; stop it from the start.

    "For rebellion is as the sin of witchcraft, and stubbornness is as iniquity and idolatry. Because you have rejected the word of the Lord, He also has rejected you from being king" (1 Samuel 15:23).

8. You are a family. Children should be included with their feelings and opinions considered on decisions. They will sometimes have some good ideas; learn to listen to them.
9. Parents, correct with authority in your voice. Children sense the tone in your voice that you mean what you say.

10. You don't just teach them, you police them. Know where your children are.

"Children learn what they live."
- If a child lives with "*Criticism*," he learns to "*Condemn*."
- If a child lives with "*Hostility*," he learns to "*Fight*."
- If a child lives with "*Ridicule*," he learns to be "*Shy*."
- If a child lives with "*Shame*," he learns to feel "*Guilty*."
- If a child lives with "*Tolerance*," he learns to be "*Patient*."
- If a child lives with "*Encouragement*," he learns "*Confidence*."
- If a child lives with "*Praise*," he learns to "*Appreciate*."
- If a child lives with "*Fairness*," he learns "*Justice*."
- If a child lives with "*Security*," he learns to have "*Faith*."
- If a child lives with "*Approval*," he learns to "*Like Himself*" (self-esteem).
- If a child lives with "*Acceptance and Friendship*," he learns to "*Give Love*" in the world.
- If a child lives with "*Good Christian Parents*," he learns to "*Love the Lord*."

101 Ways to Praise a Child

Wow, way to go; Super; You're special; Outstanding; Well done; Remarkable;

I knew you could do it; I'm proud of you; Fantastic; Superstar; Nice work;

Looking good; You're on top of it; Beautiful; Now you're flying; You're catching on; Now you've got it; You're incredible; Bravo; You're fantastic; Hooray for you; You're on target; You're on your way; How nice; How smart; Good job; That's incredible; Hot dog; Dynamite; You're beautiful; You're unique;

Nothing can stop you now; Good for you; I like you; You're a winner; Remarkable job; Beautiful work; Spectacular; You're darling; You've discovered the secret; You figured it out; Fantastic job; Hip, hip, hooray; Bingo; Magnificent; Marvelous; Terrific; Phenomenal; You're sensational; Super work; Creative job; Super job;

Fantastic job; Exceptional performance; You're a real trooper; You're responsible; You learned it right; You're exciting; What an imagination, What a good listener; You're fun; You're growing up; You tried hard; You care; Beautiful sharing; Outstanding performance; You're a good friend; I trust you; You're important; You mean a lot to me; You make me happy; You belong; You've got a friend; You make me laugh; You brighten my day; I respect you; You mean the world to me; That's correct; You're a joy; You're a treasure; You're wonderful; You're perfect; Awesome; A+ job; You're A-OK; My buddy; You made my day; That's the best;

A big hug; A big kiss; Say I Love You.

P.S. Remember, a smile is worth a thousand words.

Home Rules

- Always be honest.

    "Lying lips are an abomination to the Lord, but those who deal truthfully are His delight" (Proverbs 12:22).

- Count your blessings.

    "I will bless the Lord at all times; His praise shall continually be in my mouth. My soul shall make its boast in the Lord; The humble shall hear of it and be glad. Oh, magnify the Lord with me, and let us exalt His name together" (Psalm 34:1–3).

- Bear each other's burdens.

  "Bear one another's burdens, and so fulfill the law of Christ" (Galatians 6:2).

- Forgive and forget.

  "Who is a God like You, pardoning iniquity and passing over the transgression of the remnant of His heritage? He does not retain His anger forever, because He delights in mercy" (Micah 7:18).

- Be kind and tenderhearted.

  "And be kind to one another, tenderhearted, forgiving one another, just as God in Christ forgave you" (Ephesians 4:32).

- Comfort one another.

  "Therefore comfort one another with these words" (1 Thessalonians 4:18).

- Keep your promises.

  "And being fully convinced that what He had promised He was also able to perform" (Romans 4:21).

- Be supportive of one another.

  "I have shown you in every way, by laboring like this, that you must support the weak. And remember the words of the Lord Jesus, that He said, 'It is more blessed to give than to receive'" (Acts 20:35).

- Be true to each other.

  "They sing the song of Moses, the servant of God, and the song of the Lamb, saying: "Great and marvelous are Your works, Lord God Almighty! Just and true are Your ways, O King of the saints!" (Revelation 15:3).

- Look after each other.

    "For the poor will never cease from the land; therefore I command you, saying, 'You shall open your hand wide to your brother, to your poor and your needy, in your land'" (Deuteronomy 15:11).

- Treat each other like you treat your friends.

    "Therefore, whatever you want men to do to you, do also to them, for this is the Law and the Prophets" (Matthew 7:12).

- Most important, "*LOVE ONE ANOTHER*" deeply from the heart.

    "Since you have purified your souls in obeying the truth through the Spirit in sincere love of the brethren, love one another fervently with a pure heart" (1 Peter 1:22).

Printed in the USA
CPSIA information can be obtained
at www.ICGtesting.com
JSHW012339141123
51739JS00011B/247